SUPER
SANDCASTLE
State Stories

BUSTER'S TRIP TO CAPE COD

~ A Story About Massachusetts ~

Written by Oona Gaarder-Juntti

Illustrated by Bob Doucet

Consulting Editor, Diane Craig, M.A./Reading Specialist

ABDO
Publishing Company

Published by ABDO Publishing Company
8000 West 78th Street, Edina, Minnesota 55439.

Printed in the United States of America, North Mankato, Minnesota
112009
012010

 PRINTED ON RECYCLED PAPER

Editor: Katherine Hengel
Content Developer: Nancy Tuminelly
Cover and Interior Design: Anders Hanson, Mighty Media
Production: Colleen Dolphin, Mighty Media
Photo Credits: Colleen Dolphin, iStockphoto
(InStock Photographic Ltd., Daniel Stein, Denis Jr. Tangney),
JupiterImages Corporation, Rolf Müller, NightThree, One Mile Up,
SeaPics.com (Florian Graner), Shutterstock. Quarter-dollar coin image
from the United States Mint.

Library of Congress Cataloging-in-Publication Data

Gaarder-Juntti, Oona, 1979-
  Buster's trip to Cape Cod : a story about Massachusetts / Oona
Gaarder-Juntti ; illustrated by Bob Doucet.
    p. cm.
  ISBN 978-1-60453-921-9
  1. Massachusetts--Juvenile literature. I. Doucet, Bob, ill. II. Title.

F64.3.G33 2010
974.4'044--dc22
                              2009033789

Super SandCastle™ books are created by a team of professional
educators, reading specialists, and content developers around
five essential components—phonemic awareness, phonics,
vocabulary, text comprehension, and fluency—to assist young
readers as they develop reading skills and strategies and
increase their general knowledge. All books are written,
reviewed, and leveled for guided reading, early reading
intervention, and Accelerated Reader® programs for use in
shared, guided, and independent reading and writing activities
to support a balanced approach to literacy instruction.

TABLE OF CONTENTS

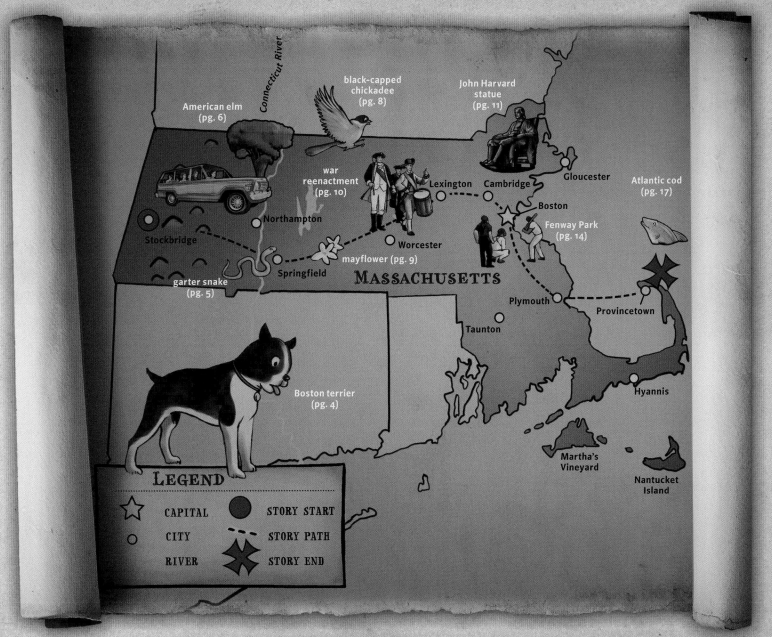

American elm (pg. 6)

Connecticut River

black-capped chickadee (pg. 8)

John Harvard statue (pg. 11)

war reenactment (pg. 10)

Lexington

Cambridge

Gloucester

Atlantic cod (pg. 17)

Northampton

Stockbridge

mayflower (pg. 9)

Worcester

Boston

Fenway Park (pg. 14)

garter snake (pg. 5)

Springfield

MASSACHUSETTS

Plymouth

Provincetown

Taunton

Hyannis

Boston terrier (pg. 4)

Martha's Vineyard

Nantucket Island

LEGEND

☆   CAPITAL   ●   STORY START

○   CITY   - - -   STORY PATH

  RIVER   ✦   STORY END

Buster's Trip to Cape Cod

Suitcases and beach toys filled the family car. They were leaving Stockbridge for a vacation in Cape Cod! Kayla and Brandon couldn't wait to see the ocean. Buster, the family's Boston terrier, was just happy to go along!

They stopped for gas and Buster looked out the window.

He saw something wiggling in the grass. He jumped out of the car and followed the movement. It was a little garter snake!

Garter Snake

The Massachusetts state **reptile** is the garter snake. Garter snakes live in forests, fields, and **wetlands**. Their bite is harmless to humans. They let out a bad smell when they are scared.

5

American Elm

The American elm is the state tree of Massachusetts. It honors George Washington's leadership during the Revolutionary War. Washington was standing under an American elm when he took command of the Continental Army. The American elm can grow up to 120 feet tall.

Gina the garter snake slithered behind an American elm. She poked her head around the tree and said, "You ssscared me! What are you doing here?"

"I'm on vacation with my family!" said Buster. But when he turned around, his family was gone.

"Oh no!" exclaimed Buster. "They left without me! I don't even know where I am!"

"Sssstay calm," hissed Gina softly. "You're in Springfield. I will help you find your family."

Springfield

Springfield is the third largest city in Massachusetts. James Naismith invented basketball in Springfield in 1891. He wanted his gym students to have something to play in the winter! The Basketball Hall of Fame is in Springfield.

Buster followed Gina through the grass. They stopped to rest near a big tree. "I wish I was in my family's car with all those beach toys," Buster said. Just then, a bird flew down from the tree.

"I saw a car full of beach toys!" said Carla the black-capped chickadee. "It looked like it was headed toward Boston. I can help you get there. I love Boston!"

Black-Capped Chickadee

The black-capped chickadee is the Massachusetts state bird. This small songbird is common throughout North America. It lives in holes in tree trunks or fence posts.

Buster said good-bye to Gina. He followed Carla down a forest trail. "You're going to love Boston," said Carla as she flew over some mayflowers. "It's a great city!" Buster was listening closely when all of a sudden they heard gunshots! He was so scared that he hid behind a tree.

Mayflower

The Mayflower became the state flower in 1918. It grows in the shade and likes sandy soil. The mayflower blooms in the spring. It is either white or pink. The mayflower is also called trailing arbutus.

Minute Man National Historical Park

The Revolutionary War started on April 19, 1775. One of the first battles took place in what is now Minute Man National Historical Park. Minutemen were Americans who were ready to fight at a moment's notice. Battle **reenactments** are often held in the park.

"Don't worry!" Carla said. "It's not a real battle. It's just a reenactment. Those park rangers aren't really soldiers. There are only dressed up like them!"

"That scared me," said Buster. "I miss my family. I wish I could find them."

Buster followed Carla to Harvard University. She showed Buster the John Harvard Statue. "Rub his foot for good luck!" explained Carla. "It works every time!" Buster rubbed the statue's foot.

"My owner Kayla is very smart. I think she wants to go to this college!" thought Buster. At that very moment, he spotted his family driving down the street!

11

"We missed them!" howled Buster.
"We'll never catch them now."

"Of course we will," said Carla. "We can take the subway to Boston!" Buster followed Carla down the stairs into Harvard Square Station. Soon, they arrived in Boston.

Boston Subway

The Boston **subway** opened in 1897. It was the first subway in America. More than 100,000 people rode it the day it opened. The Boston subway system is nicknamed The T.

Buster looked up at the tall buildings. "I've never seen anything like this!" he said.

"Now you know why I love Boston," chirped Carla. "I have to show you the baseball field! Come on!"

Carla took Buster to Fenway Park. "Strike three! You're out!" yelled the umpire. Buster looked around and noticed people eating hot dogs and other snacks. He was so hungry!

"If only I could remember where my family was going," he sighed.

"When I need to think, I go to the harbor," said Carla. "Let's try that!"

Fenway Park

Fenway Park opened on April 20, 1912. It is the oldest Major League Baseball **stadium**. It is home to the Boston Red Sox. The scoreboard is on a tall, green wall. The wall is called the Green Monster.

14

As they left the **stadium**, Buster suddenly stopped. He lifted his nose up in the air. "I smell something **delicious**, Carla!" he said. The smell was coming from a baked-bean eating contest!

Boston Baked Beans

4 cups cooked or canned navy beans

⅓ cup molasses

2 tablespoons brown sugar

1 teaspoon dry mustard

1 teaspoon ground ginger

1 teaspoon salt

¼ cup water

1 tablespoon safflower oil

1 large onion sliced into rings

Preheat oven to 350°F (176°C). Combine all the ingredients except for the oil and onion in a baking dish, along with ¼ cup of water. Mix thoroughly. Cover and bake for 30 minutes.

Heat the oil in a skillet and add the onion. Sauté until brown. After the beans have baked for 30 minutes, put the onions on top. Bake uncovered for another 10 minutes.

Carla helped Buster enter the contest. He ate as fast as he could and won! The judge placed a shiny medal around Buster's neck. "For a little dog, you sure can eat!" Carla said. "Now let's go to the harbor!"

Beantown

Native Americans taught the early settlers how to make baked beans. Years later, Boston became a major trading port for **molasses**. People started adding molasses to their baked beans! They called them Boston baked beans. That's how Boston got the nickname Beantown!

15

Boston Tea Party

When England raised the tax on tea, the American colonists got angry. On December 16, 1773, they dressed up as Mohawk Indians. Then they went onto three English ships full of tea. They dumped the tea into Boston Harbor.

They arrived at Boston Harbor and sat by the water. Buster was very sad, so Carla tried to cheer him up. "This is where the Boston Tea Party took place. Isn't that interesting?"

Just then, a fish poked his head up above the water. "It sure is!" said Kenny the cod. "This is an important place in American history!"

"That's great," said Buster. "But all I can think about is finding my family."

"Maybe I can help!" said Kenny. "Cod are very good at finding things."

"Wait!" said Buster. "Cod? That's it! My family is going to Cape Cod!"

"All right!" said Kenny. "You can catch the **ferry** in Plymouth. Follow me!"

Atlantic Cod

The Atlantic cod is the Massachusetts state fish. It is used for food and trade. An Atlantic cod can be longer than 6 feet (2 m). It weighs 11 to 26 pounds (5 to 12 kg).

17

Plymouth

Plymouth is one of the oldest towns in the United States. It is where the **Pilgrims** arrived on the Mayflower in 1620. Many **ferries**, whale watching boats, and fishing boats sail in Plymouth Harbor.

Buster ran as fast as he could to Plymouth. Just as the ferry started pulling away from shore, Buster made a giant leap off the dock.

"He made it!" cheered Carla. "Way to go, Buster!"

When the **ferry** docked at Provincetown on Cape Cod, Buster saw his family. He jumped off the ferry and ran to them. Kenny and Carla watched Buster greet his family.

"Where have you been, Buster?" his family asked. "And where did you get this medal?"

Buster just licked their faces and wagged his tail.

THE END

Cape Cod

Cape Cod is a large **peninsula** that sticks out into the Atlantic Ocean. It looks like a giant arm! Cape Cod is a very popular place for summer vacations. It has many beaches. Thousands of people visit each year!

MASSACHUSETTS AT A GLANCE

Abbreviation: MA

Capital: Boston
(20th-largest U.S. city)

Largest city: Boston

Statehood: February 6, 1788
(6th state)

Area: 10,555 sq. mi.
(27,337 sq km)
(44th-largest state)

Nickname: Bay State

Motto: Ense petit placidam
sub libertate quietem
—By the sword we seek peace,
but peace only under liberty

State bird:
black-capped chickadee

State flower: mayflower

State tree: American elm

State reptile: garter snake

State dog: Boston terrier

State insect: ladybug

State fish: Atlantic cod

State song:
"All Hail to Massachusetts"

STATE SEAL

STATE FLAG

STATE QUARTER

The Massachusetts quarter portrays
"The Minute Man," a famous statue that
stands guard at The Minute Man National
Historical Park in Concord, Massachusetts.

What Do You Know?

How well do you remember the story? Match the pictures to the questions below! Then check your answers at the bottom of the page!

a. Kenny

b. garter snake

c. Carla

d. Revolutionary War reenactment

e. Boston

f. baseball

1. What did Buster see while the family was getting gas?

2. Who helped Buster get to Boston?

3. What was happening when Buster heard the gun shots?

4. Where did Buster and Carla take the subway?

5. What did Carla and Buster watch at Fenway Park?

6. Who helped Buster remember where his family was going?

21

What to Do in Massachusetts

1 VISIT THE OLDEST SHIP IN THE US NAVY
The USS *Constitution*, Boston

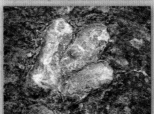

2 EXPERIENCE PREHISTORY
Dinosaur tracks, Holyoke

3 SEE A NATIONAL SYMBOL
Plymouth Rock, Plymouth

4 GO HIKING
Mount Greylock State Reservation, Lanesborough

5 VISIT A HISTORY MUSEUM
Salem Witch Museum, Salem

6 FISH FOR LOBSTERS
Rockport Harbor, Rockport

7 GO SWIMMING IN THE OCEAN
Singing Beach, Manchester-by-the-Sea

8 VISIT A FAMOUS ISLAND RETREAT
Oak Bluffs, Martha's Vineyard

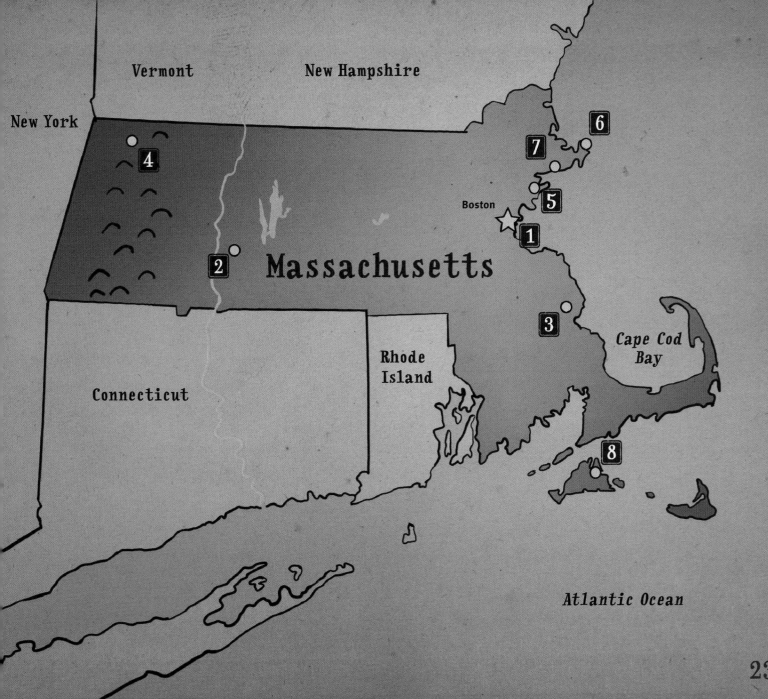

GLOSSARY

delicious – very pleasing to taste or smell.

ferry – a boat that takes people and cars across a body of water.

molasses – a thick, sweet syrup made from sugarcane.

peninsula – land that sticks out into a body of water.

Pilgrim – one of the people who came from England and started the town of Plymouth, Massachusetts.

reenactment – a performance of a historical event, such as a battle.

reptile – a cold-blooded animal, such as a snake, turtle, or alligator, that moves on its belly or on very short legs.

stadium – a large building with an open area for sporting events surrounded by rows of seats.

subway – a system of trains that run underground.

wetland – a low, wet area of land such as a swamp or a marsh.

About SUPER SANDCASTLE™

Bigger Books for Emerging Readers
Grades K–4

Created for library, classroom, and at-home use, Super SandCastle™ books support and engage young readers as they develop and build literacy skills and will increase their general knowledge about the world around them. Super SandCastle™ books are part of SandCastle™, the leading PreK–3 imprint for emerging and beginning readers. Super SandCastle™ features a larger trim size for more reading fun.

Let Us Know

Super SandCastle™ would like to hear your stories about reading this book. What was your favorite page? Was there something hard that you needed help with? Share the ups and downs of learning to read. We want to hear from you! Send us an e-mail.

sandcastle@abdopublishing.com

Contact us for a complete list of SandCastle™, Super SandCastle™, and other nonfiction and fiction titles from ABDO Publishing Company.

www.abdopublishing.com • 8000 West 78th Street
Edina, MN 55439 • 800-800-1312 • 952-831-1632 fax